The First Easter Egg

by Gina Morse
Illustrated by JSB Morse

For our beloved children, that they may seek Christ as Mary Magdalene did and find the joy of the First Easter Sunday always in their hearts.

Copyright © 2025 by Gina Morse. All Rights Reserved. Printed in the United States of America. Easter story based on John 20.

This book was produced by Libertas Kids, an imprint of Code Publishing, Covington, LA. LibertasKids.com
ISBN 978-1-60020-149-3 Ebook: 978-1-60020-150-9

On the first day of the week,
Before the sun arose,
Mary Magdalene walked in darkness,
Her heart was full of woe.

Aromatic spices in hand, she walked,
A basket of eggs, her only provision.
But when she arrived, to her surprise,
The Tomb was not what she'd envisioned.

The weighty stone which sealed the tomb
Had indeed been rolled away.
"I must go tell the others," she said.
She knew she could not stay.

The Apostles then left the tomb,
To announce what had occurred.
Mary Magdalene remained, crying,
It was still a great mystery to her!

She stooped to look inside the tomb,
What she saw, caused her fear:
Two angels sat in robes of white,
And asked the reason for her tears.

She turned around and saw a man
Who asked, "Why are you weeping?"
And again, one more question asked He:
"Whom is it that you are seeking?"

She thought He was just the gardener,
And pleaded with Him to know:
"If you took Him away, where does he lay?
Please tell me and I'll go!"

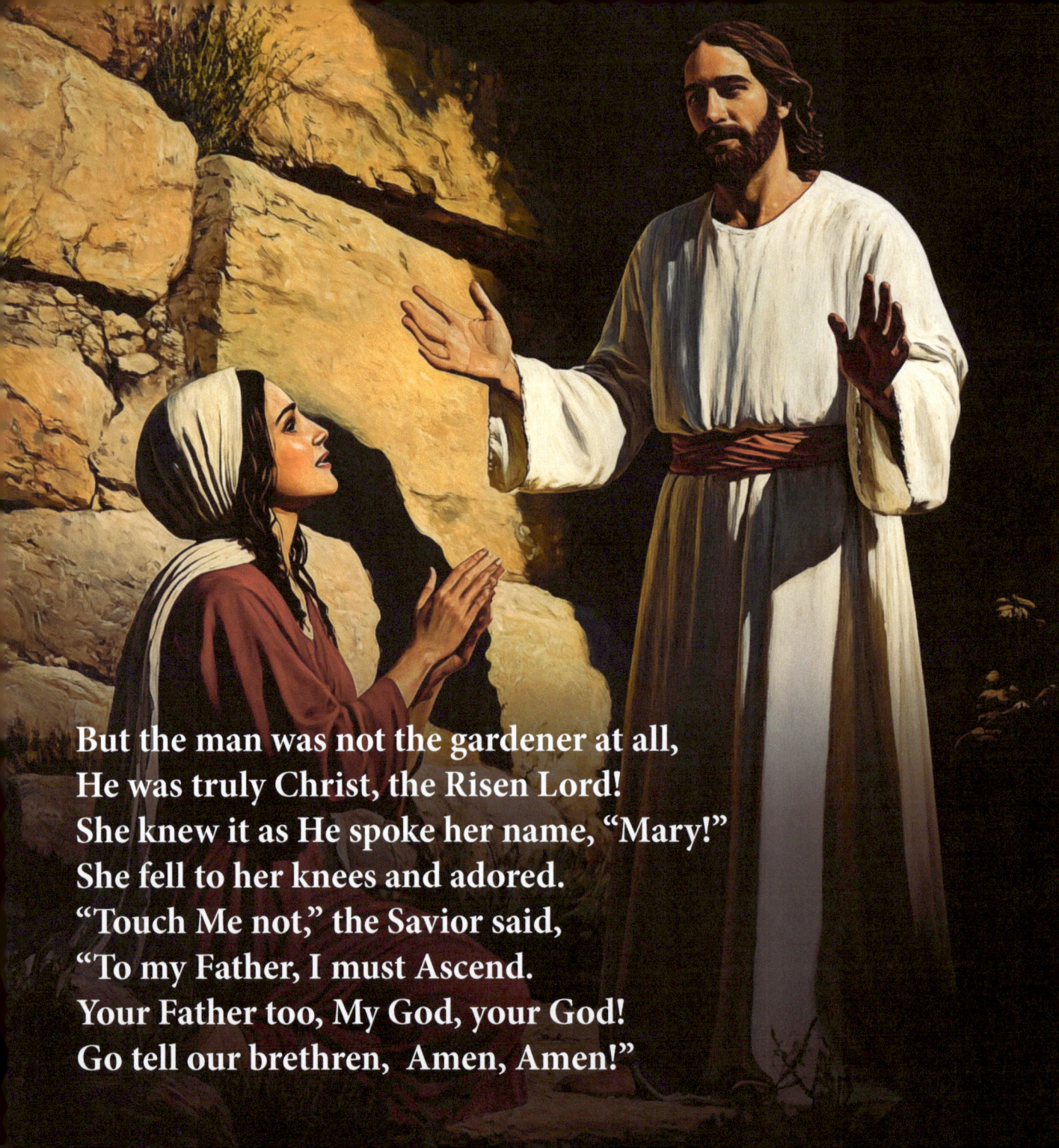

But the man was not the gardener at all,
He was truly Christ, the Risen Lord!
She knew it as He spoke her name, "Mary!"
She fell to her knees and adored.
"Touch Me not," the Savior said,
"To my Father, I must Ascend.
Your Father too, My God, your God!
Go tell our brethren, Amen, Amen!"

As she left she saw to her surprise,
The eggs once pale and white,
Now gleamed with stunning hues,
A sign of life, the Blood of Christ!

She ran to tell the world with joy,
Her voice rang strong and bright:
"Christ is risen! He lives again!
Behold, He turns death to life!"

After Christ had Ascended,
To Rome she made her way.
As was the custom, she brought a gift,
To give to the Emperor that day.

Before the proud Tiberius she stood,
Her humble gift of eggs held high.
"Christ is risen!" she proclaimed with joy,
"The Crucified One is alive!"

But as he spoke, before his eyes,
The egg blushed crimson bright.
A sign from God, so bold, so clear,
That all were astonished at the sight!

And so the news spread far and wide,
And we still tell it every Spring.
With colored eggs, a symbol of,
Jesus Christ, the Risen King.

As eggs are emptied like the Tomb,
New life will certainly come.
We remember death was conquered,
By God's Beloved Son!

THE END.

For more great stories, visit LibertasKids.com!

www.ingramcontent.com/pod-product-compliance
Lightning Source LLC
Chambersburg PA
CBHW041603070526
44586CB00003BA/65